this book belongs to

THE Better Day BOOK

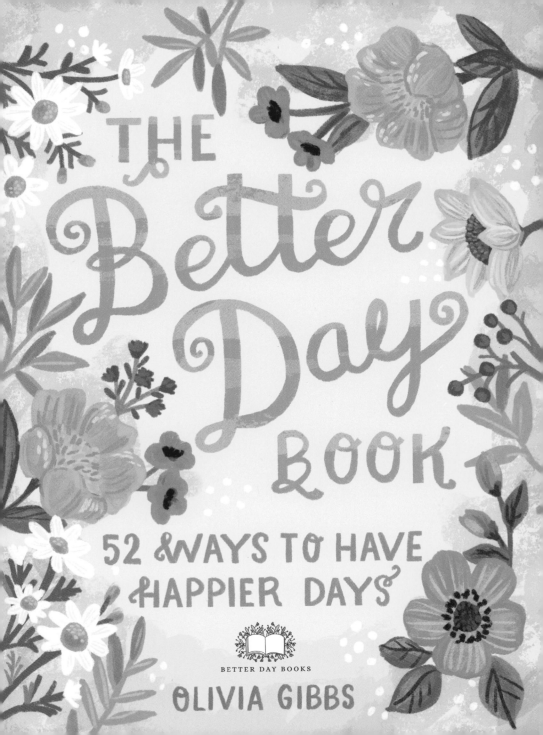

THE Better Day BOOK

52 &WAYS TO HAVE HAPPIER DAYS

BETTER DAY BOOKS

OLIVIA GIBBS

Illustrations by Olivia Gibbs
Book design by Michael Douglas

ISBN: 978-0-7643-6094-7
Printed in China
Copublished by Better Day Books and Schiffer Publishing, Ltd.

BETTER DAY BOOKS

SCHIFFER
PUBLISHING

Schiffer Publishing
4880 Lower Valley Road
Atglen, PA 19310
Phone: 610-593-1777
Fax: 610-593-2002
E-mail: Info@schifferbooks.com
Web: www.schifferbooks.com

This title is available for promotional or
commercial use, including special editions.
Contact info@schifferbooks.com for more information.

To Eva and Emma,
thank you for choosing me
to be your mom.

Contents

Welcome

Outdoors

Some ways to enjoy the outdoors and
spend more time outside.

At Home

Some ways to make your home more cozy and
comfortable so you'll love being there.

With Others

Some ways to stay connected and
enjoy time with other people.

The Little Things

Some ways to enjoy the little things in life and make your everyday routine better.

Life Is Hard

Some ways to keep a good and positive mindset when life gets challenging.

The Big Picture

Some ways to help you make big changes so you can live a more fulfilling life.

Happiness Cards

Tear and share these cards with others (or keep to yourself) to spread joy and happiness.

Welcome

I'm so happy you found this book.

I'd love to start by sharing a little bit about my self-discovery journey with you. It has taken me many years to figure out what I want to be in life and what makes my soul sparkle.

I've always loved drawing. I used to fill books and books with sketches and doodles, and I would create stories about them. But as we all do, I became an adult. I turned my back on all of my joy and creativity, dismissing it as child's play.

I grew up in a very practical family, so I decided to study business and worked in banking for many years. During that time, I was never really happy. I could feel something was missing, but I couldn't figure out what it was.

It wasn't until after the birth of my second child that my self-discovery journey really began. I started meditating, and, little by little, I noticed changes in my life. I reconnected with my creativity and passion for drawing. I became more positive and grateful for everything I had. I started making changes and noticed a big difference in my everyday life.

It is this journey that eventually led me to write and illustrate this book. I'm sharing the many ways you can make your life better too.

Working on this project was extremely fulfilling and joyous, and my biggest hope is that it helps you along on your own journey. Or at least lights a little spark in you.

Read the pages in any order you want. Some have little ideas for cheering yourself up anytime, and some have bigger ideas to help you make bigger changes. I can't wait for you to explore this collection of ideas and tips to make each day just a little bit better!

Olivia Gibbs

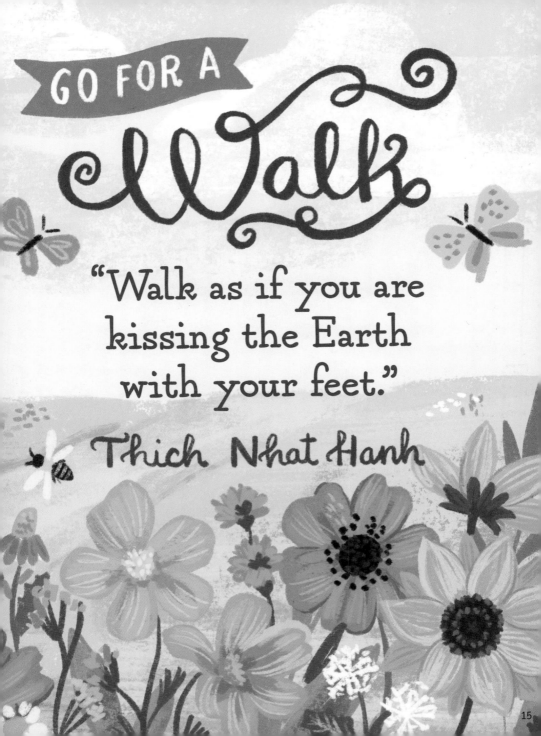

GO FOR A

Walk

"Walk as if you are kissing the Earth with your feet."

Thich Nhat Hanh

15

pick some flowers

Make a Bouquet

Dandelion

Cosmos

Poppy

Daisy

Coneflower

Spend TIME in Nature

CAMPING ESSENTIALS

Tent
Sleeping bags and pads
Little pillows
Flashlight and lanterns
Extra batteries
Camping chair and table
Water bottle
Snacks

Go ON A BIKE Ride

Soak IN THE Sun

Beach Day ESSENTIALS

Beach Bag   Sunscreen

Flip-Flops   Towel

Water Bottle   Sunglasses

Hat   Snacks

Book

Watch a Sunrise

how did they

SUNRISE:

Watch a Sunset

make you feel ?

SUNSET:

My Notes

Get MORE Sleep

SOME TIPS FOR A BETTER NIGHT'S SLEEP:

- Stick to a schedule. Go to bed and get up at the same time every day.

- Exercise during the day.

- Avoid caffeine late in the day and big meals at night.

- Follow a relaxing routine before bed. Try reading or listening to soft music.

- Avoid bright screens like the TV, the computer, or your phone.

Take a Relaxing Bath

YOU CAN ADD

Lavender   Milk

Lemons   Roses

Oranges   Honey

Oatmeal

Have 2 Plants

EASIEST INDOOR PLANTS TO GROW

- Aloe
- Succulents
- Spider Plant
- Snake Plant
- Peace Lily
- Pothos

42

OPEN THE Windows & Let the FRESH AIR IN

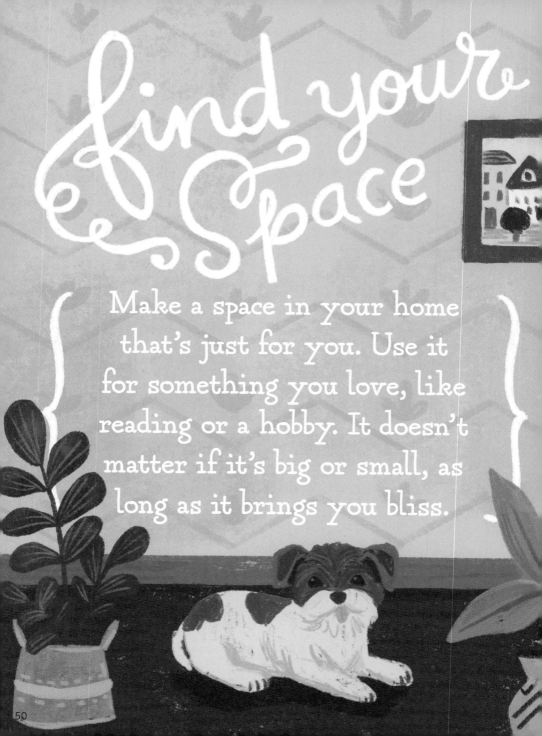

find your space

Make a space in your home that's just for you. Use it for something you love, like reading or a hobby. It doesn't matter if it's big or small, as long as it brings you bliss.

Cozy UP

ESSENTIALS

- Candles
- Blankets
- Pillows
- Plants
- Book
- Hot Drink

MY FEELINGS

natural

Read a Book

"A book is a dream you hold in your hands."
Neil Gaiman

- Books I want to read

my WISHES

TO LIVE A DREAM

My notes

& WITH

63

Go Somewhere
YOU HAVE
Never
BEEN
Before

BFF

TRIP ESSENTIALS

- ☐ Passport
- ☐ Phone (Charger)
- ☐ Water and snacks
- ☐ First aid kit
- ☐ Keep blankets in car
- ☐ Change of clothes
- ☐ Umbrella
- ☐ Sunglasses
- ☐ Sunscreen
- ☐ Maps

FIND TIME FOR Romance

SOME ROMANTIC IDEAS:

- Give your partner a full-body massage.

- Cook a romantic dinner.

- Pack a picnic and go to the park.

- Write a love letter.

- Hold hands.

- Re-create your first date.

Go out WITH YOUR friends

SOME "FRIEND DATE" IDEAS:

- Go to the movies.
- Go to a yoga class together.
- Visit a museum.
- Go for a hike.
- Bake something together.
- Go to a coffee shop.

Call Someone you Love

(NO TEXTING)

WRITE A letter TO A FRIEND WHO LIVES far away

Give
MORE
HUGS
THEY ARE LIKE

VITAMINS FOR THE SOUL

Wish OTHERS Happiness

- Something as simple as wishing others to be happy can have a great impact on your own happiness.

- Practice by secretly sending happy thoughts to someone you cross paths with during your daily routine.

My notes

Dear
Friend

Tea

Listen
TO THE
MUSIC
you
Love

Get a Massage

Different types of massage

- ☐ Swedish
- ☐ Thai
- ☐ Hot Stone
- ☐ Aromatherapy
- ☐ Deep Tissue
- ☐ Shiatsu

Treat Yourself

INDULGE IN A LITTLE PLEASURE
BY DOING SOMETHING FOR YOURSELF.
SOME THINGS YOU CAN DO:

- Buy yourself a new outfit or accessory.
- Give yourself 5 minutes to do nothing.
- Eat a decadent cake or dessert.
- Get a manicure or pedicure.

Light a CANDLE

THESE AROMAS CAN BOOST YOUR MOOD AND CREATIVITY.

Lemon

Lavender

Jasmine

Peppermint

Rosemary

Rose

Spice up your Pantry!

THESE SPICES HAVE POWERFUL HEALTH BENEFITS. TRY ADDING THEM TO YOUR FAVORITE RECIPES!

Turmeric

Parsley

Ginger

Sage

Cinnamon

Cumin

Make a Smoothie

BREW An Herbal TEA

TRY THESE SOOTHING FLAVORS.

- ☐ Chamomile
- ☐ Green Tea
- ☐ Passionflower
- ☐ Lemon Balm
- ☐ Peppermint
- ☐ Rose Tea

↪ Add honey ↩

My notes

No Rain, No Flowers

Life is a balance between bad days and good days. Just like flowers need rain to GROW, we need "rainy" days to grow too.

When Life GIVES YOU Lemons...

The difference between an obstacle and an opportunity is your attitude toward it.

...Wear them

Keep a Journal

WRITING HELPS YOU:

- Clear your mind
- Reduce stress
- Work through problems
- Know yourself better

IF OPPORTUNITY
doesn't *knock*...

Don't keep waiting for an
opportunity to come.
Get out there
and make things happen.

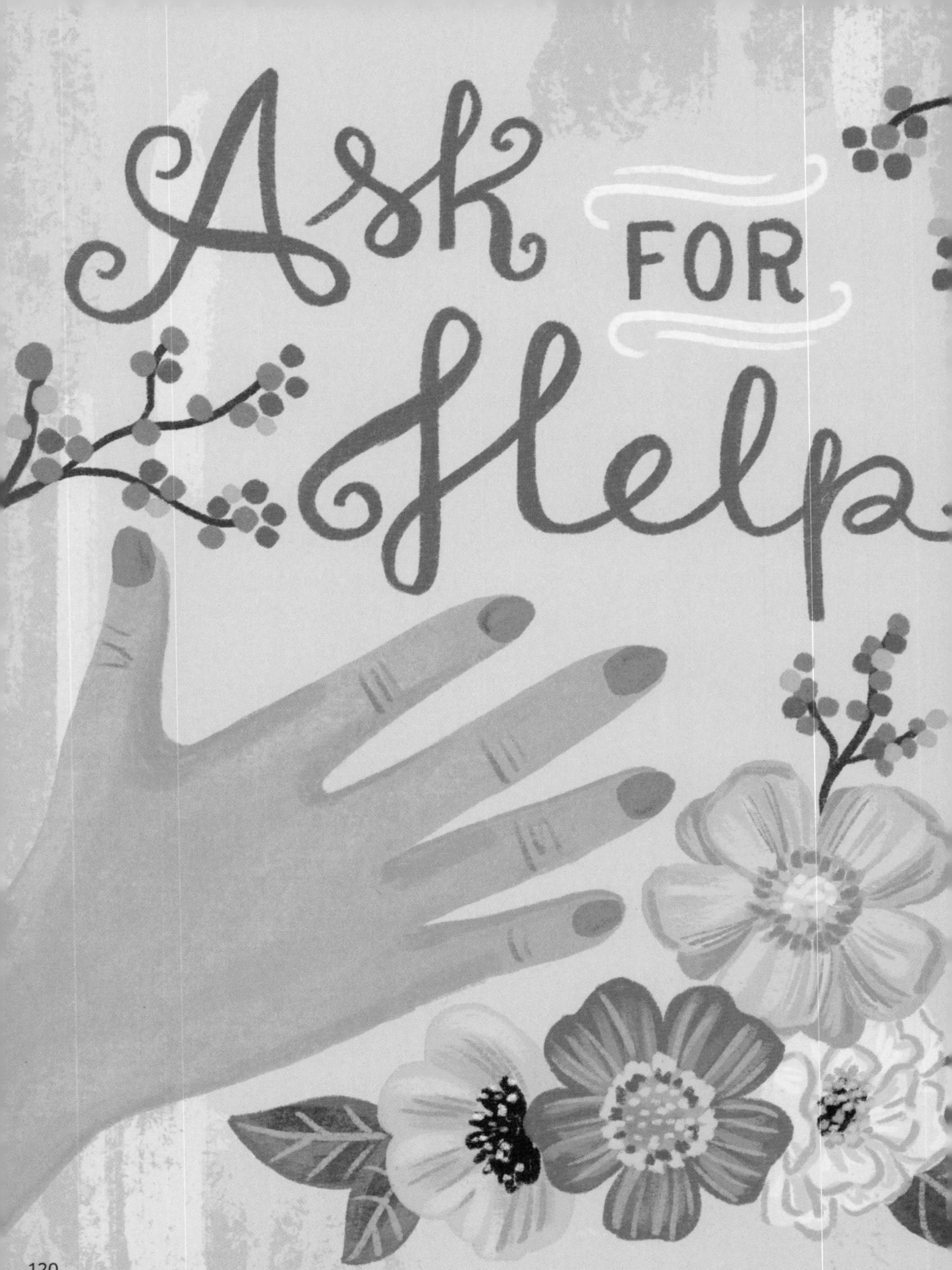
Ask FOR Help

LIST SOME WAYS
OTHERS CAN HELP:

- ☐ _____
- ☐ _____
- ☐ _____
- ☐ _____
- ☐ _____
- ☐ _____

Roll with it

Sometimes you just have to say to yourself, "It's okay. This is what's happening right now."

Roll with it

Celebrate

THERE IS ALWAYS A REASON

WRITE DOWN THE THINGS YOU HAVE
ACCOMPLISHED OR ARE PROUD OF:

O CELEBRATE

Keep Going

"Life is like riding
a bicycle. To keep
your balance,
you must keep moving."

Albert Einstein

My Notes

THE BIG

Meditate

Meditation can bring you peace and happiness by helping you change your attitude toward life.

SIMPLE TECHNIQUE

1. Sit comfortably.

2. Close your eyes.

3. Breathe naturally.

4. Focus on your breath and how your body moves when you breathe.

When you own your breath

Breathe

There are many breathing techniques you can practice. Try this one to help calm yourself and relieve stress.

1. Sit or lie down comfortably.
2. Inhale deeply through your nose for a count of 4.
3. Hold your breath for a count of 4.
4. Exhale through your nose for a count of 4.
5. Wait for a count of 4 and repeat.

nobody can steal your PEACE.

Live in the Now

Live in the Here and the Now

> Don't worry about
> the FUTURE
> or dwell on the PAST.
> Be completely aware
> of the PRESENT.

BE Grateful

Be grateful for today, and

I'M GRATEFUL FOR ...

- ☐
- ☐
- ☐
- ☐
- ☐
- ☐
- ☐

never take anything for granted.

Thanks

143

BE kind to Yourself

Accept who you are
and avoid negative self-talk.
Always talk to yourself
like you're talking to
a loved one.

KINDNESS starts with YOU

Set Goals & Visualize Them

MY GOALS:

BE Positive

{ You will attract into your life whatever you focus on. }

If you stay focused on the good
and look for the positive side of things,
you will attract more good
and positive things.

LOW HAPPINESS HIGH

DO MORE of what makes you HAPPY

Keep Dreaming

A life without

DREAMING is

A life without

MEANING

My Notes

156

ABOUT THE AUTHOR

Olivia Gibbs is an illustrator and surface pattern designer from Spain who is now based in Kansas.

Her work can be found on many different products, from greeting cards and wall art to home decor and fabric.

She lives with her husband and two daughters.

When not working on her art, she loves to travel, read, and spend time with her loved ones.

www.oliviagibbs.com

BETTER DAY BOOKS

HAPPY · CREATIVE · CURATED

Business is personal at Better Day Books. We were founded on the belief that all people are creative and that making things by hand is inherently good for us. It's important to us that you know how much we appreciate your support. The book you are holding in your hands was crafted with the artistic passion of the author and brought to life by a team of wildly enthusiastic creatives who believed it could inspire you. If it did, please drop us a line and let us know about it. Connect with us on Instagram, post a photo of your art, and let us know what other creative pursuits you are interested in learning about. It all matters to us. You're kind of a big deal.

it's a good day to have a better day!

www.betterdaybooks.com

better_day_books

TEAR & SHARE
Happiness
CARDS

In the coming pages, you will find 16 cards to tear and share.

Whether you are looking for a little pick-me-up or want to share them with a friend, these cards are sure to brighten any day.

SOME IDEAS ON HOW YOU CAN USE THEM:

- Keep them in your wallet for daily inspiration.

- Punch a hole in a corner and use them as gift tags.

- Use them to write notes and reminders.

- Leave them behind for someone random to find.

- Craft a little envelope and use them as greeting cards.

TEAR & SHARE
Happiness
CARDS